Henry VIII wanted to rule Scotland as well as England. He thought that if his son, Edward, married Mary, Queen of Scots, this would give him power over Scotland.

But some people thought that Mary, Queen of Scots should be Queen of England as well. In later years this claim was to cause problems between Queen Mary and Queen Elizabeth I of England.

MARY OF GUISE

Mary of Guise (1515-60) is best known as the mother of Mary, Queen of Scots. After the death of her husband James V in 1542, Mary stayed on in Scotland to protect her daughter's interests. She died in Edinburgh Castle.

Fast fact

A person whose job is to work out someone's family tree is called a **genealogist**. How many words can you make using the letters in the word **genealogist**?

Suggestions on page 39

The birth of Mary

Mary was born on the 8th of December 1542 in Linlithgow Palace. Only six days later she became Mary, Queen of Scots.

King James V (1512-42), the father of Mary, Queen of Scots.

ORDERS OF CHIVALRY

The present **Outer Gate** to Linlithgow Palace shows four coats of arms. These were the **orders of chivalry** to which Mary's father belonged – status symbols of their day. They were the Order of the Garter of England, Order of the Thistle of Scotland, Order of the Golden Fleece and Order of St Michael of France.

Why don't you find out more about any or all of these Orders?

Mary's father, James V, had died on 14th December, having been beaten by an English army at the Battle of Solway Moss only three weeks earlier.

Mary was still a baby and far too young to rule Scotland herself. Instead, a noble was given the job of governing Scotland until Mary was old enough to rule. He was called a **Regent**. Mary's mother wanted to be Regent of Scotland, but the job was given to the Earl of Arran. Arran was a relative of Mary, and at the time of her birth the Earl of Arran was heir to the throne of Scotland.

National Museums Scotland

... of Scots

... Douglas

... Carrie Philip

... ES EDITORS

... ordon Jarvie

Contents

Original edition published in
by HMSO publications

Published from 2000 by
NMS Enterprises Limited – F
a division of NMS Enterprise
National Museums Scotland
Chambers Street, Edinburgh

Revised and reformatted ed

Text © Elizabeth Douglas 19
Images (for © see below an

ISBN: 978-1-905267-26-2

...nging); 16 (Knox); 17
...23 (Canongate Kirk &
... & cradle); 27 (Craig-
...d); 30-31 (souvenir box
...nument); 35 (jewel);
...s' tomb [replica] by
...2, by kind permission of
... of Scotland on loan to
...otland)

... PAGE 40.

*Every attempt has been made to contact copy-
rightholders to use the material in this publication.
If any image has been inadvertently missed, please
contact the publisher.*

CARRIE PHILIP
for illustrations on pages 2-3; 4-5; 7; 10-11; 12-13;
14-15; 17; 18; 20-21; 22; 28-29; 31; front and
back cover

NATIONAL MUSEUMS SCOTLAND
(© National Museums Scotland)
for pages 5 (panel); 6 & 7 (heads); 9 (*Scotia
Regnum* map, c.1595, by Gerhard Mercator,
1512-94); 14 (Holyrood Palace); 14 (clarsach);

SCOTTIE BOOKS

For a full listing of NMS Enterprises
Limited – Publishing titles and related
merchandise:
www.nms.ac.uk/books

Mary's family tree

✓ Activity

If you would like to trace your own family tree, start by talking to family members, or look online (ask permission first) at

www.bbc.co.uk/history/ familyhistory

In the 16th century the links between the thrones of Scotland and England were very close. Mary, Queen of Scots' grandmother, Margaret Tudor, was the sister of King Henry VIII of England.

Margaret's son, James V, became ruler of Scotland when he was just two years old. As an older man, it is said that he liked to dress up as a peasant and go out into the countryside in disguise to hear what his people were saying about him.

Mary of Guise was James V's second wife. She came to Scotland from France and was part of a very important French family. James and Mary had two sons, James and Robert, who both died before their daughter, Mary, was born.

Henry VIII was King of England at the time of Mary's birth. He was also Mary's great-uncle.

Mary of Guise did not go to France with her daughter. She stayed behind in Scotland to help govern the country while Mary was abroad. But the young Queen did not travel alone. Along with adults, who looked after her, there were four little girls. These girls were to become Mary's closest friends. Their names were Mary Seton, Mary Beaton, Mary Livingston and Mary Fleming.

The French King sent his own royal ship, along with a hundred others, to fetch Mary to France. They took a route which avoided places where they might meet English ships. On 7th August 1548 Queen Mary sailed from Dumbarton, leaving Scotland for the first time.

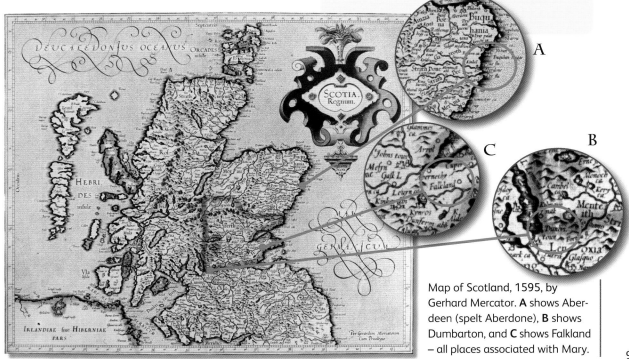

Map of Scotland, 1595, by Gerhard Mercator. **A** shows Aberdeen (spelt Aberdone), **B** shows Dumbarton, and **C** shows Falkland – all places associated with Mary.

Mary's life in France

THE ARMES OF ALLIACE BETVIX THE DOLPHIN OF FRANCE AND MARIE QVENE OF SCOTLAND

Queen Mary arrived in France on the 13th of August 1548. She travelled through the north of the country to a castle where the French royal children were staying.

Queen Mary and Dauphin Francis (1544-60).

The castle was based at Carrières near Saint-Germain. It was there that Mary met her future husband, the Dauphin Francis, for the first time. (**Dauphin** was the title given to the heir to the throne of France.) He was a small, pale boy of four. Mary liked Francis from the start and treated him like her little brother.

AULD ALLIANCE

Those living in Scotland between 1513 and 1560 had the privilege of also being deemed citizens of the kingdom of France. This was granted by the French king.

The **Auld Alliance** between France and Scotland created important social and trade links that lasted for over 300 years. The *Garde Ecossaise* was a company of Scots archers who once guarded the French kings.

Queen Mary and the Dauphin were officially engaged on 11th April 1558. Their wedding took place two weeks later at Notre-Dame Cathedral in Paris. Mary was 15 and Francis 14. Mary wore a beautiful white dress with lots of sparkling jewellery. After the marriage, Mary became known as **Queen Dauphiness**.

For a year Mary led a happy life as Queen Dauphiness, but this was soon to change as three tragedies touched her life one after the other.

Découvrir / To find out

Many Scottish towns and cities are twinned with French towns. Look out for road signs as you enter a town. Is your town or city twinned with one in France?

King Henry II of France died in June 1559. He had been taking part in a jousting tournament and was fatally wounded. As a result, Mary became Queen of France as well as Queen of Scotland. Then, on 11th June 1560, Mary's mother, Mary of Guise, died in Edinburgh. Finally, at the end of that dreadful year, Francis died on the 5th of December. Returning home from a day's hunting he complained of earache. This turned into a more serious illness from which he did not recover.

Mary now had a very difficult decision to make. Should she stay in France or return to the country of her birth? She was visited in France by her half-brother, Lord James Stewart. He brought with him an invitation for her to return to Scotland from the lords who were governing the country. Mary decided it was time to return to her homeland to rule Scotland herself.

Return to Scotland

On a misty August morning in 1561 two French galley ships sailed into Leith harbour. On one of the ships was Mary, Queen of Scots. It was 13 years since Mary had lived in Scotland, and there was no one waiting to meet her ....

The ships had arrived much earlier than expected. While they waited for the official party of welcome, Mary was shown into the house of a rich merchant called Andrew Lamb. A messenger was quickly sent to Lord James Stewart, to inform him that the Queen had arrived.

When the Queen's party finally travelled through the streets of Edinburgh to Holyrood Palace, the people of the city cheered when they saw Mary, a tall, beautiful woman dressed in black.

A ROYAL WELCOME

The east coast haar that shrouded Edinburgh on Mary's return was said by the preacher John Knox (see pp. 16-17) to be the frown of God! Mary was still only a teenager of 18 years, yet she was a widow and a stranger in her homeland. How do you think she must have felt on her return home?

The painting opposite shows Mary wearing a traditional black gown of a widow in mourning. But black was also a striking and fashionable colour in those days.

Flag alphabet

What message do the flags on the French galleys have for the Scottish people? Use the flag alphabet on the opposite page to find out.

Answer on page 39

A B C D E F G H I J K L M N O P Q R S T U V W X Y Z

Mary and her 'Four Maries'

Mary Seton, Mary Beaton, Mary Livingston and Mary Fleming returned from France with Queen Mary and became her ladies-in-waiting at Holyrood Palace.

The first evening Queen Mary was back in Scotland, a crowd of Edinburgh people sang songs and played music for her out-side the gates of Holyrood Palace. They came back for a few nights after that too. The people seemed very pleased that their Queen had come home.

Mary had many ways of keeping amused during the evenings in Holyrood Palace. She enjoyed billiards, backgammon, chess and cards. She also liked to dress up in disguise. On one occasion the Queen and her 'Maries' dressed up as merchants' wives and went out unrecognised into the streets of Edinburgh.

Right: This instrument is a **clarsach**, or Highland harp, given by Queen Mary to a lady in Banchory, Aberdeen-shire, after a hunting trip.

HOLYROOD PALACE

Fast fact

In the parkland around Arthur's Seat, near Holyrood, Mary hunted, went riding and hawked. She even played golf.

Mary also performed plays using her own set of puppets. Some evenings were spent in the company of her 'Four Maries', playing games, music, or working on her embroidery.

?
Mystery object

Do you know what the game is on the left? This was a gift given to Mary Seton from her Queen.

Answer on page 39

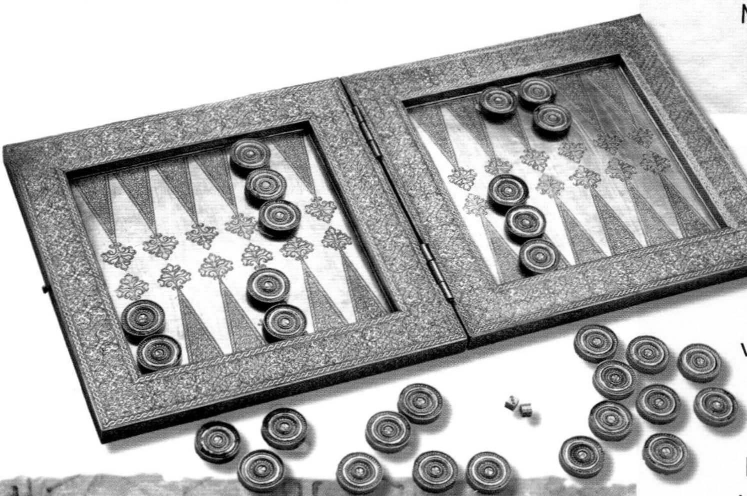

Embroidery

Below is a wool hanging from Linlithgow Palace with velvet appliqué work. It is a metre wide and a metre and a half long. Needlework was a favourite pastime for court ladies and Mary was highly skilled at embroidery.

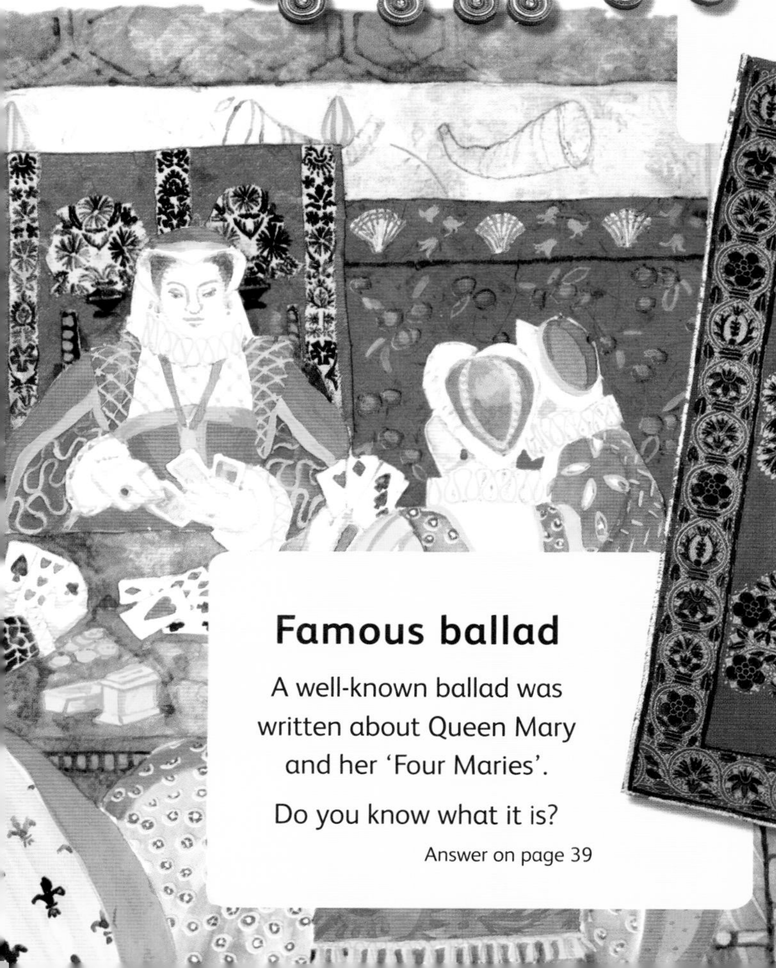

Famous ballad

A well-known ballad was written about Queen Mary and her 'Four Maries'.

Do you know what it is?

Answer on page 39

Queen Mary and Knox

When Queen Mary returned to Scotland in August 1561 most people were overjoyed to see her. But there was one man who did not share their joy. He was called John Knox.

Knox is said to be buried under Parliament Square in the High Street of Edinburgh. It used to be the burial ground of St Giles Kirk, where he was minister.

Knox was a Protestant preacher and a leading member of the new Protestant or Reformed Church. While Mary was in France there had been great religious changes in Scotland. Many were unhappy with the Roman Catholic Church, the Church of the Stewart monarchs. Among these people were a group of leading Scottish noblemen, including Mary's kinsman, Lord James Stewart.

Knox had joined the Protestant Church which had grown very popular during the years of Mary's absence. On 17th August 1560 the Protestant Church became the official Church in Scotland.

Roman Catholics who stayed faithful to their Church had to worship in private as the public saying of Mass was banned. As Mary was a devout Roman Catholic, Knox was not happy to see her back because he did not want Scotland to return to the Catholic Church.

An engraving of the Protestant preacher, John Knox.

Look it up

Test your knowledge on the **Renaissance** and **Reformation** at the following website:

www.bbc.co.uk/history/scottishhistory

Write your own short definitions of **Renaissance** and **Reformation**.

Mary tried to deal with the difficult issue of religion soon after her return. She said that Protestantism could remain in Scotland, but she wanted to be able to follow her own Catholic faith in private. This did not satisfy Knox, who preached a fiery sermon making very clear his thoughts about the Catholic Church. This led to his first stormy meeting with the Queen. They met four more times, usually after Knox had preached a sermon that Mary disagreed with.

Above, right: John Knox House in the High Street, Edinburgh. Below: A battle of wits between Knox and his Queen.

JOHN KNOX

Born in Haddington *c*.1514, Knox studied at St Andrews University. One surprising fact is that Knox was a galley slave for almost two years, when taken prisoner in 1547 after the siege of St Andrews Castle. It is thought that he knew about the plan to murder David Riccio (see pages 22-23).

17

Mary's travels

In August 1562 Queen Mary decided that she would like to make a **progress**, or royal tour, of the north of Scotland ....

On 12th August 1562 the Queen set out from Holyrood Palace. A few of the places she visited before reaching Aberdeen were Linlithgow, Stirling, Perth and Glamis.

But Mary had another reason for visiting the north of Scotland. One of the noble families of that area was causing trouble. The Earl of Huntly, a Catholic, thought that the Queen was being too nice to the Protestants in Scotland and said so in public.

He was also angry that Mary had recently granted the title of Earl of Moray to her half-brother, Lord James Stewart. The new Earl of Moray's land bordered on to Huntly's land. Huntly had made a lot of money from this land in the past, and now it had been given to someone else. He was very angry.

Huntly's son, John Gordon, was also a problem for Mary. He had committed a crime in Edinburgh and had escaped from prison. So the Queen was not very pleased with either the Earl of Huntly or his wayward son.

Advice for travellers

On Queen Mary's tours nearly everything was packed up after the royal stay and taken to the next palace: household goods, beds, bedding, small pieces of furniture, luxury items, tapestries – and even the windows!

After visiting Inverness the Queen returned to Aberdeen, closely followed by John Gordon who had a plan to kidnap the Queen and to marry her.

At Aberdeen the Queen received some worrying news – the Earl of Huntly was gathering an army. He too was ready to march to Aberdeen, kidnap the Queen and marry her to whomever he wanted. Mary was furious and sent for her own troops so that she could deal with the troublesome Earl of Huntly and his son.

On 28th October 1562 at Corrichie, near Aberdeen, the Earl of Moray and the Earl of Maitland led the Queen's army into battle. The battle was won quickly by the Queen's army, and Huntly and his son were taken prisoner. Soon after, the Earl of Huntly collapsed and died.

John Gordon was put on trial in Edinburgh. This time he was found guilty of treason and executed.

Mary, Queen of Scots' coat-of-arms at Falkland Palace, Fife.

FALKLAND PALACE

Falkland Palace, Fife, was one of Mary's favourite places to visit. From the **Burgh Seal** of Falkland (left), which sport do you think the Queen enjoyed in the Forest of Falkland?

Answer on page 39

Anyone for tennis?

Another sport popular in Mary's time was **Royal Tennis**. It is one of the most difficult ball games to play. The Falkland Palace tennis court is the oldest in Britain. Mary would have loved the challenge.

Lord Darnley

Bronze medal of Queen Mary and Lord Darnley, struck in honour of their marriage in 1565.

On her return to Scotland in 1561, Queen Mary knew that she had a difficult job ahead.

After a year of ruling the country on her own, she decided that it was time she got married again. Mary needed someone to help her govern Scotland.

Mary's first choice for a new husband was Don Carlos, heir to the Spanish throne. This would have given Scotland a powerful friend and ally. This choice, however, did not please Queen Elizabeth of England, who had other ideas. Elizabeth hinted that if Mary accepted *her* choice of husband, she would consider making the Scottish Queen heir to the throne of England. This was something that Mary wanted above all else.

First of all, Elizabeth suggested her own courtier Robert Dudley, the Earl of Leicester, as a suitable marriage partner. However, in February 1565 Mary met another young man from England. He was Henry Stewart, Lord Darnley, a tall and fair-haired youth with fine courtly manners. Darnley was a cousin of Queen Mary. His father was the

Earl of Lennox and his mother was Lady Margaret Douglas. Mary and Darnley shared the same grandmother, Margaret Tudor, sister of Henry VIII of England.

Queen Mary still had not made a decision about who should be her new husband, but Don Carlos could no longer be considered because he was very ill. Although disappointed about this news, worse was to come. A message arrived from the English Queen telling Mary that even if she did choose the Earl of Leicester, she would not become heir to the English throne. Mary was very, very angry at this news and turned all her attention to Lord Darnley.

As time went by it became clear that Lord Darnley was not as nice a person as he had first appeared. He was a proud and moody man. Many people tried to persuade Mary not to marry him, but by then she had made up her mind.

Queen Mary and Lord Henry Darnley were married on 29th July 1565 at Holyrood Palace. The service was held at six o'clock in the morning. Darnley left the chapel after the main service was over. As he was a Protestant, he did not stay to hear Mass with the Queen. In the afternoon a big wedding reception was held for Queen Mary and her new husband in the Palace.

At the wedding banquet

The Queen would have been served with four helpings of each dish – one to eat and the rest to be given to the poor.

Cooks might have used the following ingredients for special meals:

capon, catfish, eels, goose, mutton, oysters, partridge, perch, pigeon, pike, porpoise, salmon, snails, toadfish, venison and wild boar. (Lots of herbs and spices were also used to disguise any food that had gone off!)

Which of these foods would we *not* eat today?

Answers on page 39

The murder of Riccio

Lord James Stewart, the Earl of Moray.

Perhaps Queen Mary should have listened to her friends when they advised her not to marry Lord Darnley, for her life became more difficult from the day of their wedding.

The Queen's half-brother, James Stewart, and her husband, Darnley, did not like each other. The problems between them became so bad that Lord James and some of his friends were forced to leave Scotland.

Queen Mary decided that James Stewart and his friends should have their lands taken from them for the trouble they had caused. The Scottish Lords, loyal to Lord James, were angry and decided to take matters into their own hands. They planned to involve Darnley in the murder of the Queen's secretary, David Riccio.

Riccio (also spelt Rizzio) was an Italian who joined Mary's court in 1561. Always ambitious, he worked his way up through the Queen's household to become her private secretary in 1564. The Lords, angry about the exile of James Stewart, did not like Riccio. He had been given far too much power for someone from his background.

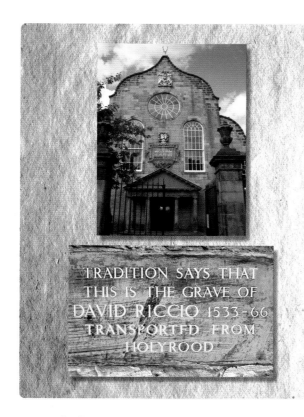

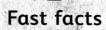

Fast facts

If you go on a tour of Holyrood Palace, Edinburgh, look out for the small door-way and stairs which Darnley and the other Lords used on the night of David Riccio's murder. It is next to the entrance which leads into the Queen's bed chamber.

You can also visit the nearby cemetery at Canongate Kirk (left) on the Royal Mile, Edinburgh, where there is a plaque that marks the place where Riccio is supposedly buried.

First of all, the Lords encouraged Darnley to believe he was being unfairly treated by the Queen – Darnley wanted more power than Mary was prepared to give him. Then they started a rumour that Mary was getting far too friendly with David Riccio. The plan worked and soon Darnley became so annoyed with his wife that he agreed to take part in the murder of her secretary.

By the beginning of March 1566, Mary was living very quietly at Holyrood. She was expecting a baby in June and could not go out as often as before. On the evening of 9th March, Mary and her friends were sitting in the Queen's private rooms in Holyrood Palace. Riccio was with

them. They were just about to eat when a noise came from the stairs leading from the Queen's rooms. The curtain moved and Darnley came in, followed swiftly by some other men. Darnley held the Queen aside while the others murdered David Riccio, stabbing him 56 times. Mary was extremely angry and upset.

The next day Darnley came to her to say he was sorry for what had happened. He told her that, following Riccio's murder, the Lords planned to take her to Stirling Castle and hold her there until her baby was born. The Queen forgave Darnley for his part in the murder and decided to leave Holyrood Palace for both her own safety and that of her unborn child.

The birth of Prince James

With the help of a group of loyal friends, Queen Mary and Darnley escaped from Holyrood Palace a few days after Riccio's murder.

They left in the middle of the night and headed for Dunbar Castle. Queen Mary and Darnley returned to Edinburgh on 18th March at the head of a large army. By the time they reached the city, David Riccio's murderers had already fled.

Mary no longer felt safe in Holyrood Palace, so she moved into Edinburgh Castle. It was there on 19th June 1566

Right: A gold and enamel locket with tiny miniatures inside of Mary, Queen of Scots and her son, James VI.

Burgh life in Mary's time

Visit the website at:

www.bbc.co.uk/scotland/education/ as/burghlife

Complete the quiz and you can attend the christening banquet of Mary's son, Prince James.

that the Queen gave birth to a baby boy. He was called James, named after the Queen's father. The whole of the country rejoiced. Now there was an heir to the throne of Scotland.

Later on, in the summer of that year, Mary went stag-hunting at Traquair in Peeblesshire in the company of a group of noblemen. John Stewart, the Laird of Traquair, was the captain of the Queen's guard at Holyrood Palace; he had helped Mary to escape after Riccio's murder.

Cradle said to have been used by Queen Mary for her son, James.

Places to visit

If you visit Queen Mary's House in Jedburgh (right), you will find objects reputedly connected with Mary, Queen of Scots, including this miniature (below, right).

In Traquair House there is a rosary and crucifix belonging to Mary.

The cradle used by Queen Mary for her son James and a cameo locket (see opposite page) are currently in the National Museum of Scotland.

By this time the Queen and her husband were not getting on very well and Darnley did not join the Queen stag hunting until later in the summer. When he did arrive he argued with Mary all the time and was very unkind to her.

In October 1566 Queen Mary went on a royal tour of the Scottish border towns. While visiting Jedburgh, she became very ill. The people with her thought she might die. It was only the quick thinking of the Queen's French doctor that saved her life and helped her to get well again.

Edinburgh Castle as it was before the 1570s. Here, in 1566, Mary gave birth to Prince James.

Kirk o' Field

When Queen Mary returned to Edinburgh she decided to stay at Craigmillar Castle, on the outskirts of the city. There she held a meeting with a group of the most important Scottish Lords.

Henry Stewart, Lord Darnley (1545-67). Darnley was Consort of Mary, Queen of Scots, but he had no royal powers.

They talked about Lord Darnley and his behaviour. It was not the way a King of Scotland should conduct himself. At the christening of Prince James, Lord Darnley's actions were particularly bad. The christening took place on 17th December 1566 in the Chapel Royal in Stirling Castle. But Darnley did not agree with Mary's choice of godparents for his son, so he refused to attend the ceremony. Instead he left Stirling for Glasgow, where he became seriously ill.

Mary decided that she would try to sort out the problems between herself and her husband. When Darnley returned to Edinburgh on 1st February 1567 he stayed in a house at Kirk o' Field, just inside the city walls, intending to remain there until he was completely well. On Sunday 9th February, Mary visited him to see if he was well enough to return to Holyrood Palace.

That day the Queen was very busy. One of her servants was getting married and she had an important dinner to go to in the afternoon. In the evening the Queen went to visit Darnley at Kirk o' Field. She would have liked to stay longer with her husband but she was reminded that she had to return to the Palace. The Queen was due to attend the evening's entertainment at her servant's wedding.

Around two o'clock in the morning Edinburgh was shaken by a loud explosion.

Fast fact

It is thought that Darnley may have been ill with small-pox, which is highly infectious. Mary had small-pox as a child, but it left no visible scars. Do you know which scientist helped to wipe out this disease?

Answer on page 39

The explosion came from the direction of Kirk o' Field. The first people to arrive saw that the house had been blown up and destroyed. People searched among the ruins, but found no sign of the Queen's husband. Eventually the bodies of Darnley and his servant were discovered in the garden at the back of the house. It looked as if they had been trying to escape. There were no marks on their bodies to show that they had been in an explosion, and they may have been strangled or suffocated.

The houses at Kirk o' Field stood where the Edinburgh University buildings are located today at the corner of Chambers Street and the South Bridge in Edinburgh city centre. Below is a contemporary drawing of the explosion.

Fast fact

The area in the shadow of Craigmillar Castle is still known as Little France because Mary kept a few French servants to remind her of her happy years in that country. Below is Craigmillar Castle as it looks today.

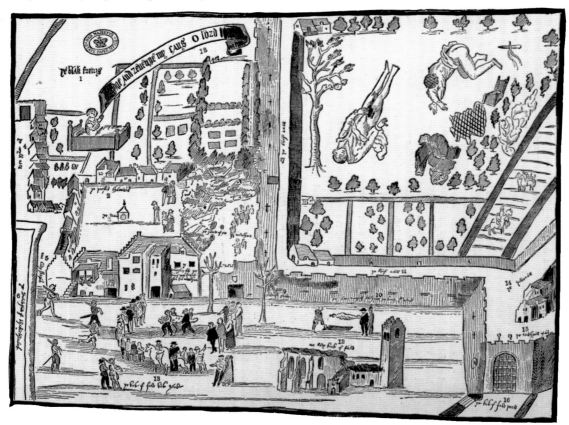

27

The Earl of Bothwell

There was one Scottish nobleman who was always at Queen Mary's side during this troubled time. He was James Hepburn, the Earl of Bothwell.

James Hepburn (*c*.1535-78), the 4th Earl of Bothwell.

The Queen valued his help, but many people did not trust him. They thought he was to blame for the explosion at Kirk o' Field. The Queen was warned, by her friends, of what people might think if she became too friendly with Bothwell. Posters began to go up around Edinburgh linking the Queen and Bothwell with Darnley's murder. And the Earl turned out to have plans of his own, as he intended to marry Queen Mary.

On 20th April 1567 Queen Mary and her courtiers travelled to Stirling Castle to visit the baby Prince James. Stirling Castle served as the nursery for many Scottish royal children and James was to spend most of his childhood there. The Queen's return journey was brought to a halt by a band of men led by Bothwell. He kidnapped the Queen and took her and a few of her courtiers to Dunbar Castle.

Mary and the Earl of Bothwell returned to Edinburgh on 6th May 1567. On 15th May they were married in Holyrood Palace, even though barely three months had passed since the death of Lord Darnley, the Queen's second husband.

Left: The ruins of Dunbar Castle.

The other Scottish Lords thought that Bothwell was hardly a suitable husband for Queen Mary. They also did not like the fact that he had kidnapped her. The Lords decided it would be best if Bothwell was punished, so they took their soldiers and marched to Borthwick Castle where Queen Mary and her new husband were staying. The castle was surrounded by the Lords' army. Mary and Bothwell made a plan. While the Queen spoke to the Lords, Bothwell escaped. Then, in the middle of the night, Mary herself escaped from the castle dressed as a man. Bothwell and Mary met up again at Dunbar Castle.

The Queen realised that she was in danger of losing her throne, so she began to gather her own army. At Carberry, just outside Musselburgh, on 15th June 1567, the Queen's army met the Lords' army. The Lords demanded that if the Queen wanted the country to return to normal she would have to leave Bothwell. Faced with this stark choice, the Queen persuaded Bothwell to flee.

Queen Mary went back to Edinburgh with the Lords, but this time she was greeted with shouts and jeers from people as she entered the city. Mary now realised that she was the Lords' prisoner, and instead of being taken to Holyrood Palace she was shut away in a small room at the Provost of Edinburgh's house.

Lochleven Castle

The Lords had tricked Queen Mary into leaving Bothwell in exchange for her freedom, but she was now their prisoner.

From the Provost of Edinburgh's house, Mary was taken briefly to Holyrood Palace and then on to the island castle of Lochleven near Kinross. Lochleven Castle was the home of the Douglas family.

Queen Mary was very ill during her first few weeks on the island. People thought that she might die. It was during the Queen's illness that she was forced to sign abdication papers. This meant that Mary had given up her throne. On 29th July 1567 Prince James was crowned King of Scotland. King James VI was just over one year old. The Queen's half-brother, Lord James Stewart, the Earl of Moray, became Regent.

Mary never gave up hope that one day she might be free again, and there were people in the castle willing to help her. Two friends that the Queen made in the castle were George and Willie Douglas.

George was the brother of the Laird of Lochleven. Willie was a poor relative of the family who worked as the Laird's personal servant.

Mary first tried to escape from Lochleven Castle towards the end of March 1568 and left the island disguised as a washer woman. It was the Queen's fine hands that gave her away. The boatman took the Queen back to the island, but he was a kind man and did not tell anyone what had happened. Mary's second attempt, however, was more successful and she escaped from Lochleven Castle on 2nd May 1568, with the help of George and Willie Douglas.

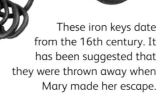

These iron keys date from the 16th century. It has been suggested that they were thrown away when Mary made her escape.

Mary left the castle in disguise, by the postern gate. Willie Douglas led everyone in a game of 'The Lord of Misrule' (like 'Follow my Leader') to stop people noticing that there were horsemen gathering on the shore. Then he stole the keys to the castle. The castle gates were locked at seven o' clock each evening. No guards were on duty after that time. Willie rowed the Queen across the Loch where George Douglas waited with a horse ready for her escape.

Your escape plan

George and Willie Douglas' escape plan was very clever. If you had been a prisoner in the castle, think about how you might have escaped.

(Remember, Mary was trapped in a cramped tower in a corner furthest from the shore. It would have been impossible for her to signal for help.)

The Battle of Langside

Queen Mary wanted her throne back. The Scottish nobles who had helped the Queen escape from Lochleven Castle were soon joined by others.

At the head of a large army, Queen Mary marched to Glasgow where the Regent Moray was staying. She knew that she would have to defeat him if she wanted her throne back.

The Regent came to meet the Queen with his own soldiers. His army was smaller than Mary's, but more organised. The two sides met at a village called Langside, just south of Glasgow, on 13th May 1568.

As the battle was about to begin, one of Mary's generals fainted. His men fled and there was confusion in the rest of the army. The Queen went among the men to encourage them, but they were arguing with each other. Mary could see that she had lost the battle and fled, heading for the south-west of Scotland where people were still loyal to her.

Langside Heritage Trail

The **Langside Heritage Trail** in Glasgow features many royal connections. Look out for the **Langside Monument** (see below) which commemorates the final defeat of Queen Mary. Many local street names are called after those who fought in the Battle. **Queen's Park**, for example, is named after Mary, Queen of Scots. It was designed by Joseph Paxton who also designed Kelvingrove Park. **Battlefield Rest** was once one of the finest tram shelters in Glasgow!

Mary mourning over the dying George Douglas at the Battle of Langside. George had helped her to escape from Lochleven Castle (see pages 30-31).

With the help of her followers, Queen Mary left Scotland on 16th May 1568 for the second and last time. She was still only 26 years old.

Fast fact

Queen Mary spent her last night in Scotland at Dundrennan Abbey. She disguised herself this time by cutting her hair and wearing plain clothes.

Mary had decided to ask the English Queen for help. Elizabeth had sent messages of support during Mary's imprisonment in Lochleven Castle, and at this point Mary was still hopeful that her fortunes would change. Little did she know that she was to spend the rest of her life as a prisoner.

... also on the Trail

This is a detail of stained glass at Rawcliffe, Mansionhouse Road, on the **Langside Trail**. It is the road's grandest house and was, until recently, a convent run by Carmelite nuns. Indeed the area is known as 'Vatican Hill' because of this and other religious buildings in the area.

Queen's Park Rose Garden

Visit the Scottish Poetry Rose Garden created in 2003. It is designed in the form of a thistle. Mary wrote poetry during her time in captivity in Fotheringay Castle (see page 37). ('Fotheringay' is sometimes spelt 'Fotheringhay'.)

33

England's royal prisoner

Mary, Queen of Scots had come to England looking for help, but instead she was made a prisoner ....

Queen Mary and her supporters landed at Workington on the English coast at seven o'clock in the evening. The next day the Deputy Governor of Carlisle Castle and a hundred soldiers arrived to escort the Queen to Carlisle. At Carlisle she was watched by guards at all times.

Mary had expected some assistance from Elizabeth, but the English Queen refused to see her. Elizabeth did not really want to help Mary because she still felt very threatened by the Scottish Queen who had always wanted to rule England herself. Elizabeth was well aware that some of her own subjects thought that Mary should be Queen of England instead of her. So rather than meeting with Mary straight away, Elizabeth said that she would see her when all the suspicions

Royal graphology

When young, Mary was taught the new Italian style of handwriting, and she signed her name in the French form, 'Marie Stuart'.

What do you notice about the letters?

Answer on page 39

Right: Elizabeth I of England (1533-1603). Just as Mary was born 'Mary Stewart' from the Royal Stewart line of monarchs, Elizabeth was born 'Elizabeth Tudor' from the House of Tudor.

Right: This jewel is a late 16th-century cameo enamelled locket which contains an image of Mary, Queen of Scots.

surrounding the murder of Mary's husband, Lord Darnley, had been cleared and her innocence in the murder proven.

Mary was given the chance to defend her name at a meeting in York in October 1568. Mary's half-brother, Lord James Stewart, the Earl of Moray, was also at the meeting, and he wanted to prove that both Queen Mary and Lord Bothwell were involved in Darnley's murder.

Moray had one important piece of evidence which he thought would prove that the charge was true. He claimed that he had a box which belonged to Lord Bothwell. This box was supposed to contain letters from the Queen to Bothwell which told of Lord Darnley's murder. These letters became known as the 'Casket Letters', but they were thought to be forgeries.

Elizabeth sent a group of noblemen to listen to the evidence from both sides, but they were unable to reach a decision one way or the other. Mary meanwhile remained a prisoner of the English.

Fast fact

The box which contained the 'Casket Letters' can be seen at Lennoxlove House, outside Haddington. Lennoxlove is now the home of the Duke of Hamilton.

Anagrams

Here are some places in Scotland connected with Mary, Queen of Scots. Unscramble the letters to work them out:

XNEOLELVON ◆ IOILLTHWGN
GLINRIST ◆ BINERDUGH
EELVOCNLH ◆ BNADMORUT

Answers on page 39

Mary's trial and execution

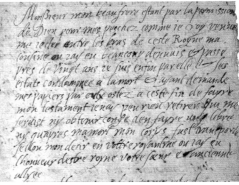

Mary's last letter was written in French to King Henri III of France, on the eve of her execution in February 1587.

For the next 19 years, from 1568 to 1587, Mary was moved from one prison to another within England. Mary Seton was allowed to stay with her Queen, to help look after her.

There were several failed plots to free Mary from her prison. One of them set out to make Mary the Queen of England instead of Elizabeth. Elizabeth was very worried about this. She did not want to lose her throne and so she gave her 'spy-master', Sir Francis Walsingham, the task of finding out the names of her enemies.

Walsingham particularly wanted to catch Mary plotting against his own Queen.

After the last failed plot, Mary was not allowed to write any letters. As this had been her only means of keeping in touch with the outside world, she was very pleased when someone agreed to carry letters for her in secret. But that person was working for Walsingham and any letters Mary wrote or received were shown to Sir Francis before being delivered to their intended reader. Mary did not suspect that her letters, which had been so cunningly hidden in a beer barrel, were being read by Francis Walsingham. This is how the **Babington Plot** was discovered. A group of young English noblemen, including the Catholic Sir Antony Babington, planned to free Mary and make her Queen of England instead of Elizabeth. All they needed was Mary's agreement.

During her time in prison Mary hoped that one day her son, James VI of Scotland, would rescue her. But James had been brought up by his tutor George Buchanan to hate and fear his mother, so he did not try to set her free. In July 1586 Mary received bad news. James had signed a peace treaty with Elizabeth and would receive money from her in return. This made Mary very upset. She wrote a letter to Babington, agreeing to his plans. Reading the letter, Walsingham realised he now had Mary in his trap.

The trial

Queen Mary's trial began on 15th October 1586 in Fotheringay Castle. She was charged with plotting to kill Queen Elizabeth. Mary spoke in her own defence because she was not allowed a lawyer. Found guilty of treason, she was sentenced to be executed.

The execution and afterwards

Early in the morning of 8th February 1587, Mary, Queen of Scots was executed in the Great Hall at Fotheringay Castle, Northamptonshire. When Queen Elizabeth I of England died in 1603, King James VI of Scotland became King of England too. He felt sad and possibly guilty about the way that his mother had been treated. He had Fotheringay Castle demolished and Mary's body moved to a marble tomb in Westminster Abbey.

Mary, Queen of Scots' tomb replica at the National Museum of Scotland in Edinburgh. The original tomb is in Westminster Abbey in London. It was made by Cornelius Cure between 1606 and 1612.

The word search grid:

```
P A T O U C A N R B
H A Y F J A N E U D
E E L L Q T G H N R
A L F L S I T M I E
S E R I T U X O C I
A P E A W O Z N O N
N H T N R A A K R D
T A T S I V M E N E
C N U N O I L Y P E
G T B E A V E R E R
```

Mary's embroidery

To pass the time while being kept prisoner, Queen Mary did a lot of embroidery. You can see a piece of her work in Holyrood Palace, Edinburgh. The ideas for the pictures came from books of animals and plants. The images would be copied on to canvas before being embroidered.

Word search

Hidden in this word search are the names of 14 creatures that Queen Mary may have included in her embroidery.

Can you find them? (You can move diagonally, as well as up and down, and in any direction.)

Answers on page 39

ANSWERS

Page 3: **Fast fact** – If you found over 50 words, well done! There could be more. You can also include plurals. Suggestions include: age, agonise, along, angel, angle, atone, eagle, elongate, gale, gate, gene, genial, gin, gist, glean, glisten, goal, goalie, gone, is, isle, it, lane, late, line, list, listen, log, long, longest, lost, nail, neat, negate, nil, sag, sane, seal, sign, signal, sin, sing, single, singlet, slogan, stain, stale, steal, stole, stone, sting, tan, tangle, teal, teen, ten, toe, tone ….

Page 5: **I-spy** – Spot the unicorns on pages 5, 19 and 38. Unicorns are often used in heraldry; two unicorns support the Scottish arms. It is a mythical animal with the head of a horse, beard of a goat, legs of a deer, tail of a lion, and, of course, the legendary horn.

Page 7: **The Coronation** – Pearls are also special because they symbolise purity. In ancient times it was said that they were formed by drops of rain falling into open oyster shells.

Page 9: **Detective work** – A 'bonspiel' is a curling match. Teams meet from all over Scotland for a North *versus* South tournament.

Page 9: **Nursery rhyme** – *Mary, Mary quite contrary / How does your garden grow? / With silver bells and cockleshells / And pretty maids all in a row*. Some people believe that this rhyme may be about Mary, Queen of Scots. The 'pretty maids' may refer to her 'Maries'. Others believe that the rhyme refers to Mary I of England (1516-58), daughter of Henry VIII and half-sister of Elizabeth I who became Queen after Mary's death.

Page 12: **Flag alphabet** – The message in flags on the French galley reads 'Long live Queen Mary'.

Page 15: **Mystery object?** – This is a late 16th-century silver-gilt gaming board used for backgammon, 'nine-men-morris', draughts or chess, with silver pieces and gold dice. It was a gift from Queen Mary to one of her most loyal friends, Mary Seton.

Page 15: **Famous ballad** – *Yestreen the Queen had four Maries, / The nicht she'll hae but three; / There was Mary Seton and Mary Beaton … / And Mary Carmichael and me* (chorus). You will find the whole ballad in a book. Ballads often have many versions with different characters, stories and spellings. The tale told here is not strictly accurate.

Page 19: **Falkland Palace** – Mary enjoyed hunting.

Page 21: **At the wedding banquet** – Most of the foods listed are still eaten today, but *not* the porpoise which is a protected species! And capons and snails don't feature in modern British menus.

Page 26: **Fast fact** – In the 1790s the English scientist Edward Jenner noticed that milkmaids affected by cow-pox did not then develop small-pox. Jenner created a vaccine to prevent small-pox occurring.

Page 34: **Royal graphology** – First, it is interesting to note that Mary signed her name 'Marie R' ('Marie' is the French form of Mary, and R is for the Latin word '*Regina*' or Queen). 'Italian style' writing is also called 'Italic script'. It slopes neatly down from right to left.

Page 35: **Anagrams** – LENNOXLOVE, LINLITHGOW, STIRLING, EDINBURGH, LOCHLEVEN, DUMBARTON

Page 38: **Word search** – You will find the following creatures in the word search: an ape, beaver, butterfly, cat, eel, elephant, lion, monkey, pheasant, reindeer, snail, tiger, toucan and unicorn.

FACTS AND ACTIVITIES – ANSWERS

Page i: **Mary's writing** – English translation: 'Your very humble and very obedient daughter, Mary'.

Page iv: **Life in the 16th century** – It is worth noting that we know a lot more about those at the Royal Court during this time than we know about ordinary people. Wealthy people could afford portraits, and were able to write, so they left some evidence of fashion and lifestyle. But, as clothes and possessions were re-used until they wore out, little has survived to tell us how poorer folk lived.

The Royal Court:
– Court dress for men and women would have been made of fine and expensive materials, such as lace, damask, silver cloth, silks and satins, and often from foreign sources.
– Look at page 21 to see what those at Court might have been served at the banquet.
– Look at pages 14-15 to see what kinds of entertainment those at Court might enjoy.
– Work at Court might involve governing the country, making laws, or looking after the Queen.

The High Street, Edinburgh:
A tailor would have used wool and coarser cloth for his less wealthy customers who might have worn rough sarks (shirts), plaids and breeches.
– Oats for porridge or gruel, barley, fish, vegetables, pulses, herbs, and anything that could be grown was more typical for ordinary people. Meat, particularly beef, was important for Scots, rich or poor, which was unusual in Europe at that time. Adults and children drank beer because the water was so foul.
– In the High Street the lure of the tavern, or street entertainers like pipers, might keep your mind off the long hours of work.
– They may work as tailors, furriers, glovers, coopers (barrel-makers), bonnet-makers, seamstresses or souters (shoe-makers), among other jobs.

ANSWERS (cont'd)

Page v: **French and Scots word search** – Answers below:

```
A A W C O U P F H R I E J L C
C A D D I E D O U C E M S B V
H A B H H X J U I S V T S H
O S E I M O G V H M D W A H U
U H Z M X G W V A D D N N A P
L E A O U M Q T U S O F K R P
E T Y O Q A Z G O R H C U M W
T E N L O N Y R I W A S Z U T
F I D Y X A U P R T D W R H C
Y S Q D H Y W E O H E I H O Y
E S E R E G V G E O S M E H E
S A P A T Y I T C B B A C U U
U T J G S J B O U L S P R L T
A M I V V B E J A N T D C B B
C F R F O G J V I I R R X I M
```

Page viii: **Mary of Guise's House** – This door would have been found on the outside of the house. Such skilled and ornately carved coats of arms would have been expensive and are a sign of wealth.
– There is no letter-box, for example, and today we do not tend to put hinges on the outside of a door.

PLACES OF INTEREST

The following places in Scotland are associated with Mary, Queen of Scots. They are either places where she stayed, or have items of interest relating to her. Remember, as opening times vary it would be useful to check details with local Tourist Information Offices.

DUMBARTON: Dumbarton Castle
DUMFRIES AND GALLOWAY: Dundrennan Abbey
EAST LOTHIAN: Lennoxlove House
EDINBURGH: Craigmillar Castle, Edinburgh Castle, Holyrood Palace, John Knox House, National Museum of Scotland, Scottish National Portrait Gallery
FIFE: Falkland Palace
KINROSS: Lochleven Castle
SCOTTISH BORDERS: Mary, Queen of Scots' House, Jedburgh
PEEBLESSHIRE: Traquair House
STIRLING: Stirling Castle; Inchmahome Priory, Lake of Menteith
WEST LOTHIAN: Linlithgow Palace

RELATED WEBSITES

Remember, ask permission before you use the internet.

BBC   www.bbc.co.uk/familyhistory
www.bbc.co.uk/scottishhistory

Historic Scotland
www.historic-scotland.gov.uk

National Museums Scotland
www.nms.ac.uk

National Trust for Scotland
www.nts.org.uk

Scottish National Portrait Gallery
www.nationalgalleries.org

FURTHER CREDITS

CASSELL'S *OLD AND NEW EDINBURGH: Its History, its People, and its Places* by James Grant (Cassell & Company Ltd: London, Paris, New York and Melbourne) (no date) – for illus. on pages 16 (Knox burial marker); 25 (Edinburgh Castle); art section viii (Mary of Guise door)

THE COMPREHENSIVE HISTORY OF ENGLAND: Civil, Military, Religious, Intellectual and Social by Charles Macfarlane and Rev. Thomas Thomson (Blackie & Son: Glasgow, Edinburgh & London) (no date) – for illus. on pages 8 (Henry VIII); 28 (Dunbar Castle); 34 (Elizabeth I); art section i (Mary, Queen of Scots); art section ii (Henry VIII, Elizabeth I, Mary, Queen of Scots and James VI); art section iii (Royal Arms of England assumed by Mary, Queen of Scots); art section iv (contemporary fashion)

FRANCES AND GORDON JARVIE – for page 19 (Falkland Palace)

GLASGOW MUSEUMS (THE BURRELL COLLECTION) (© Culture and Sport Glasgow [Museums]) – for page 13 (*Mary, Queen of Scots, 1685*, by unknown artist)

HISTORIC SCOTLAND (© Crown copyright reproduced courtesy of Historic Scotland) – for illustrations on pages 4 (Outer Gate. Linlithgow); 5 (fountain); 7 (Crown Jewels)

LENNOXLOVE HOUSE (In the collection of Lennoxlove House Limited, Haddington © 2012) – for page 35 (casket)

THE LIBRARY OF CONGRESS (Prints and Photographs Division, Washington DC 20540, USA) – for pages 6 (Stirling Castle, 1890-1900); 8 (Dumbarton Castle, 1890-1900); 33 (Mary mourning Douglas)

MARY, QUEEN OF SCOTS AFTER THE BATTLE OF LANGSIDE for page 33 (stained glass window in Rawcliffe Mansion, Langside, by W. & J. J. Kier, Glasgow, 1874). See also Langside Heritage Trail information and Glasgow City Council.

NATIONAL GALLERIES OF SCOTLAND (SCOTTISH NATIONAL PORTRAIT GALLERY) – for pages 3 (*Mary of Guise, 1515-60. Queen of James V*, by Corneille de Lyon [presented by E. P. Jones]; 4 (*James V, 1512-42. Father of Mary, Queen of Scots*, by unknown artist); 26 (*Henry Stewart, Lord Darnley, 1545-67, Consort of Mary, Queen of Scots*, by unknown artist); 28 (*James Hepburn, 4th Earl of Bothwell, c.1535-78. Third husband of Mary, Queen of Scots*, by unknown artist); 37 (*The Execution of Mary, Queen of Scots, 1542-87*, by unknown artist)

NATIONAL LIBRARY OF SCOTLAND (© National Library of Scotland) – for pages 10 (*Mary, Queen of Scots and the Dauphin Francis*, Adv. Ms 31.4.2 f.19); 36 (*Last letter of Mary, Queen of Scots*, Adv. Ms. 54.1.1 ff.1r., 2v)

THE NATIONAL TRUST FOR SCOTLAND (© The Trustees of the National Library of Scotland) – for page 19 (seal and Royal Tennis)

SCOTTISH BORDERS COUNCIL (© Scottish Borders Council Museums & Galleries Service) – for page 25 (Mary, Queen of Scots' House and miniature of Mary)

Mary, Queen of Scots
Facts and activities

Vostre treshumble ex tresobeissante fille
Marie

This book belongs to:

_____

Write your name on the above line.
(Try to copy Mary's writing above, or as it appears on page 34. Although the image is of Mary as an adult, this piece of script was written when she was just eight years old. She was writing to her mother in the French language. Do you know what it says? The answer is on page 39.)

European rulers

Scotland		England	
AD **1460**	James III	**1485**	Henry VII
1488	James IV		
1513	James V	**1509**	Henry VIII
1542	Mary (Stewart) (Her mother, Mary of Guise, rules as Regent from 1554, after the Earl of Arran)	**1547**	Edward VI
		1553	Mary (Tudor)
		1558	Elizabeth I
1567	James VI (becomes James I of England on the death of Elizabeth I in 1603)		
1603	James VI becomes I of England	**1603**	James I (VI of Scotland)

HENRY VIII

ELIZABETH I

MARY, QUEEN OF SCOTS

JAMES VI AND I

France		Spain		The Popes	
1483	Charles VIII	1474	Isabella and Ferdinand	1484	Innocent VIII
				1492	Alexander VI
1498	Louis XII				
				1503	Pius III
				1503	Julius II
1515	Francis I	1516	Charles I	1513	Leo X
				1522	Adrian VI
				1523	Clement VII
				1534	Paul III
1547	Henry II			1550	Julius III
		1556	Philip II	1555	Marcellus II
1559	Francis II			1555	Paul IV
1560	Charles IX			1559	Pius IV
				1566	Pius V
				1572	Gregory XIII
1574	Henry III			1585	Sixtus V
1589	Henry IV				
				1590	Urban VII
				1590	Gregory XIV
				1591	Innocent IX
		1598	Philip III	1592	Clement VIII
1610	Louis XIII	1621	Philip IV	1605	Paul V

Life in 16th-century Scotland

When Mary returned to Scotland from France, she had her Royal Court in Holyrood Palace, Edinburgh. But life for those at the Court was very different to life for ordinary people at that time.

Do some historical research. Find books in your school library, or your local library, or get permission to use the internet, or visit a museum in your area which has 16th-century objects. Keep a note of what you discover about the following aspects of life at that time (suggestions on page 39).

The Royal Court

♦ Imagine you are expected to attend the Royal Court. What might you wear?

♦ Today the Queen is holding a banquet in honour of a visiting French diplomat. What might you expect to eat?

♦ What entertainment will you fill your hours with?

♦ What work do you do; and what other jobs might be done at court?

Remember that life might be very different for men and women, wealthy or not!

The High Street, Edinburgh

♦ You are a tailor living in one of the crowded closes or streets in Edinburgh's High Street. What might your less wealthy customers wear?

♦ You have finished your work for the day as a busy seamstress mending clothes for your wealthy neighbours. What food might you have to prepare a meal for your family?

♦ You have so little time off because you work such long hours. What would you like to do if you had spare time?

♦ What do the people in your street do for a living?

French and Scots word search

Many French words have survived in the Scots language. The phrase 'Dinna fash yerself!', for example, comes from the French word *fâcher*, meaning to trouble or inconvenience someone.

Try out this word search. You can move diagonally, as well as up and down, in any direction, to find the listed words. Use a Scots dictionary to find out what they mean.

Answers on page 40

ASHET	CAUSEY	GARDYLOO	IGOT
BEJANT	COUP	HOGMANAY	STANK
BOULS	DOUCE	HOULET	SYVER
CADDIE	FASH	HOWTOWDIE	TASSIE

Move diagonally, as well as up and down, in any direction, to find the following words:

A	A	W	C	O	U	P	F	H	R	I	E	J	L	C
C	A	D	D	I	E	D	O	U	C	E	M	S	B	V
H	A	B	H	H	H	X	J	U	I	S	V	T	S	H
O	S	E	I	M	O	G	V	H	M	D	W	A	H	U
U	H	Z	M	X	G	W	V	A	D	D	N	N	A	P
L	E	A	O	U	M	Q	T	U	S	O	F	K	R	P
E	T	Y	O	Q	A	Z	G	O	R	H	C	U	M	W
T	E	N	L	O	N	Y	R	I	W	A	S	Z	U	T
F	I	D	Y	X	A	U	P	R	T	D	W	R	H	C
Y	S	Q	D	H	Y	W	E	O	H	E	I	H	O	Y
E	S	E	R	E	G	V	G	E	O	S	M	E	H	E
S	A	P	A	T	Y	I	T	C	B	B	A	C	U	U
U	T	J	G	S	J	B	O	U	L	S	P	F	L	T
A	M	I	V	V	B	E	J	A	N	T	D	C	B	B
C	F	R	F	O	G	J	V	I	I	R	R	X	I	M

v

Race for the throne

Mary
flees to England and is imprisoned by Queen Elizabeth.
Miss a turn.

Mary
is put on trial for her part in the 'Babington Plot'.
Miss a turn.

Mary
is imprisoned in Lochleven Castle and gives up the throne to her son James, who becomes King of Scotland on 29th July 1567.
Miss a turn.

Mary
is found guilty and is executed on 8th February 1587.
Miss a turn.

Go back one space.

Carberry clash
between the Queen's army and that of the Scottish Lords, 15th June 1567. Bothwell flees. Mary is taken prisoner by the Lords.
Miss a turn.

Lord Darnley
is murdered in Kirk o' Field, Edinburgh, in February 1567.
Miss a turn.

Toss the coin again!

Lord Bothwell
and Queen Mary are married on 15th May 1567.
Miss a turn.

Prince James
is born on 19th June 1566.
Move forward one space.

David Riccio
is murdered in the Queen's presence in March 1556.
Miss a turn.

THE END
JAMES BECOMES KING OF ENGLAND IN 1603

This is a game for 2 to 4 players. You will need a coin. You will also need a small counter for each player. Follow the instructions on the spaces you land on.

To move, toss the coin:
Heads = move 2 spaces
Tails = move 1 space
The winner is the player who reaches the throne first!

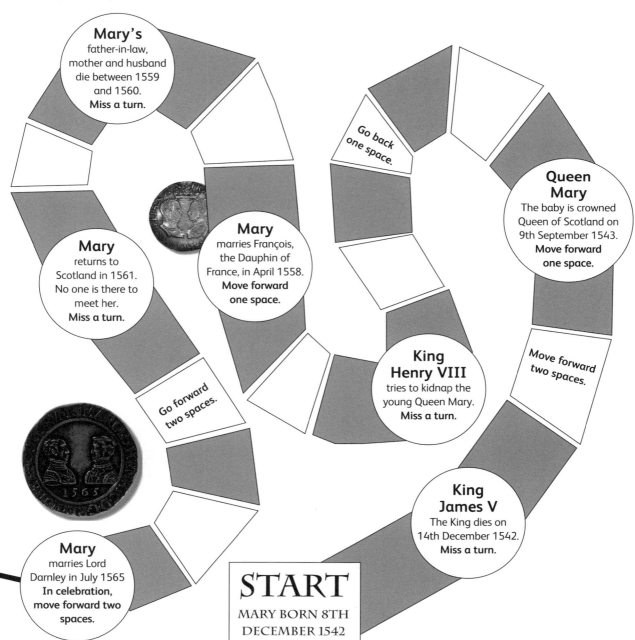

Mary's father-in-law, mother and husband die between 1559 and 1560. **Miss a turn.**

Mary returns to Scotland in 1561. No one is there to meet her. **Miss a turn.**

Mary marries François, the Dauphin of France, in April 1558. **Move forward one space.**

Go back one space.

Queen Mary The baby is crowned Queen of Scotland on 9th September 1543. **Move forward one space.**

Move forward two spaces.

King Henry VIII tries to kidnap the young Queen Mary. **Miss a turn.**

Go forward two spaces.

Mary marries Lord Darnley in July 1565 **In celebration, move forward two spaces.**

King James V The King dies on 14th December 1542. **Miss a turn.**

START

MARY BORN 8TH DECEMBER 1542

Mary of Guise's House

It is thought that Mary's mother, Mary of Guise, stayed in a house in Blyth's Close, Edinburgh, between 1542 and 1554.

This is a door from the original house. It is made of oak and richly carved with people, animals and coats of arms, although it is thought that the coats of arms were later additions. The door can be seen in the National Museum of Scotland, Edinburgh.

- Do you think that this door would have been found on the outside of the house, or the inside? And why?

- Think of your own front door – are there any things missing from this door when compared to a modern one? See suggestions on page 40.

- You can create your own carving design in the frame below.